D1554431

When I Was Dead
and Other Stories

Vincent O'Sullivan

When I Was Dead and Other Stories

Copyright © 2012 by Indo-European Publishing

Contact:
IndoEuropeanPublishing@gmail.com

The present edition is a reproduction of 1921 publication of this work, produced in the current edition with completely new, easy to read format by Indo-European Publishing.

For an authentic reading experience, the Spelling, punctuation, and capitalization have been retained from the original text.

Cover Design by Indo-European Design Team

ISBN: 978-1-60444-626-5

IndoEuropean
Publishing.com
Los Angeles, CA, USA

Table of Contents

When I Was Dead

"And yet my heart
Will not confess he owes the malady
That doth my life besiege."
—All's Well that Ends Well

That was the worst of Ravenel Hall. The passages were long and gloomy, the rooms were musty and dull, even the pictures were sombre and their subjects dire. On an autumn evening, when the wind soughed and ailed through the trees in the park, and the dead leaves whistled and chattered, while the rain clamoured at the windows, small wonder that folks with gentle nerves went a-straying in their wits! An acute nervous system is a grievous burthen on the deck of a yacht under sunlit skies: at Ravenel the chain of nerves was prone to clash and jangle a funeral march. Nerves must be pampered in a tea-drinking community; and the ghost that your grandfather, with a skinful of port, could face and never tremble, sets you, in your sobriety, sweating and shivering; or, becoming scared (poor ghost!) of your bulged eyes and dropping jaw, he quenches expectation by not appearing at all. So I am left to conclude that it was tea which made my acquaintance afraid to stay at Ravenel. Even Wilvern gave over; and as he is in the Guards, and a polo player his nerves ought to be strong enough. On the night before he went I was

1

explaining to him my theory, that if you place some drops of human blood near you, and then concentrate your thoughts, you will after a while see before you a man or a woman who will stay with you during long hours of the night, and even meet you at unexpected places during the day. I was explaining this theory, I repeat, when he interrupted me with words, senseless enough, which sent me fencing and parrying strangers,—on my guard.

"I say, Alistair, my dear chap!" he began, "you ought to get out of this place and go up to Town and knock about a bit—you really ought, you know."

"Yes," I replied, "and get poisoned at the hotels by bad food and at the clubs by bad talk, I suppose. No, thank you: and let me say that your care for my health enervates me."

"Well, you can do as you like," says he, rapping with his feet on the floor. "I'm hanged if I stay here after to-morrow I'll be staring mad if I do!"

He was my last visitor. Some weeks after his departure I was sitting in the library with my drops of blood by me. I had got my theory nearly perfect by this time; but there was one difficulty. The figure which I had ever before me was the figure of an old woman with her hair divided in the middle, and her hair fell to her shoulders, white on one side and black on the other. She as a very complete old woman; but, alas! she was eyeless, and when I tried to construct the eyes she would shrivel and rot in my sight. But to-night I was thinking, thinking, as I had never thought before, and the eyes were just creeping into the head when I heard terrible crash outside as if some heavy substance had fallen. Of a sudden the door was flung open and two maid-servants entered they glanced at the rug under my chair, and at that they turned a sick white, cried on God, and huddled out.

"How dare you enter the library in this manner?" I demanded sternly. No answer came back from them, so I started in pursuit. I found all the servants in the house gathered in a knot at the end of the passage.

"Mrs. Pebble," I said smartly, to the housekeeper, "I want those two women discharged to-morrow. It's an outrage! You ought to be more careful." But she was not attending to me. Her face was distorted with terror.

"Ah dear, ah dear!" she went. "We had better all go to the library together," says she to the others.

"Am I master of my own house, Mrs. Pebble?" I inquired, bringing my knuckles down with a bang on the table.

None of them seemed to see me or hear me: I might as well have been shrieking in a desert. I followed them down the passage, and forbade them to enter the library.

But they trooped past me, and stood with a clutter round the hearth-rug. Then three or four of them began dragging and lifting, as if they were lifting a helpless body, and stumbled with their imaginary burthen over to a sofa. Old Soames, the butler, stood near.

"Poor young gentleman!" he said with a sob. "I've knowed him since he was a baby. And to think of him being dead like this and so young, too!"

I crossed the room. "What's all this, Soames!" I cried, shaking him roughly by the shoulders. "I'm not dead. I'm here—here!" As he did not stir I got a little scared. "Soames, old friend!" I called, "don't you know me! Don't you know the little boy you used to play with? Say I'm not dead, Soames, please, Soames!"

He stooped down and kissed the sofa. "I think one of the men ought to ride over to the village for the doctor, Mr. Soames," says Mrs. Pebble; and he shuffled out to give the order.

Now, this doctor was an ignorant dog, whom I had been forced to exclude from the house because he went about proclaiming his belief in a saving God, at the same time that he proclaimed himself a man of science. He, I was resolved, should never cross my threshold, and I followed Mrs. Pebble through the house, screaming out prohibition. But I did not catch even a groan from her, not a nod of the head, nor a cast of the eye, to show that she had heard.

4

I met the doctor at the door of the library. "Well," I sneered, throwing my hand in his face, "have you come to teach me some new prayers?"

He brushed by me as if he had not felt the blow, and knelt down by the sofa.

"Rupture of a vessel on the brain, I think," he says to Soames and Mrs. Pebble after a short moment. "He has been dead some hours. Poor fellow! You had better telegraph for his sister, and I will send up the undertaker to arrange the body."

"You liar!" I yelled. "You whining liar! How have you the insolence to tell my servants that I am dead, when you see me here face to face?"

He was far in the passage, with Soames and Mrs. Pebble at his heels, ere I had ended, and not one of the three turned round.

All that night I sat in the library. Strangely enough, I had no wish to sleep nor during the time that followed, had I any craving to eat. In the morning the men came, and although I ordered them out, they proceeded to minister about something I could not see. So all day I stayed in the library or wandered about the house, and at night the men came again bringing with them a coffin. Then, in my humour, thinking it shame that so fine a coffin should be empty I lay the night in it and slept a soft dreamless sleep—the softest sleep I have ever slept. And when the men came the next day I rested still, and the undertaker shaved me. A strange valet!

On the evening after that, I was coming downstairs, when I noted some luggage in the hall, and so learned that my sister had arrived. I had not seen this woman since her marriage, and I loathed her more than I loathed any creature in this ill-organised world. She was very beautiful, I think—tall, and dark, and straight as a ram-rod—and she had an unruly passion for scandal and dress. I suppose the reason I disliked her so intensely was, that she had a habit of making one aware of her presence when she was several yards off. At half-past nine o'clock my sister came down to the library in a very charming wrap, and I soon found that she was as insensible to my presence as the others. I trembled with rage to see her kneel down by the coffin—my coffin; but when she bent over to kiss the pillow I threw away control.

A knife which had been used to cut string was lying upon a table: I seized it and drove it into her neck. She fled from the room screaming.

"Come! come!" she cried, her voice quivering with anguish. "The corpse is bleeding from the nose."

Then I cursed her.

On the evening of the third day there was a heavy fall of

snow. About eleven o'clock I observed that the house was filled with blacks and mutes and folk of the county, who came for the obsequies. I went into the library and sat still, and waited. Soon came the men, and they closed the lid of the coffin and bore it out on their shoulders. And yet I sat, feeling rather sadly that something of mine had been taken away: I could not quite think what. For half-an-hour perhaps— dreaming, dreaming: and then I glided to the hall door. There was no trace left of the funeral; but after a while I sighted a black thread winding slowly across the white plain.

"I'm not dead!" I moaned, and rubbed my face in the pure snow, and tossed it on my neck and hair. "Sweet God, I am not dead."

The Bargain of Rupert Orange

Chapter I

The marvel is, that the memory of Rupert Orange, whose name was a signal for chatter amongst people both in Europe and America not many years ago, has now almost died out. Even in New York where he was born, and where the facts of his secret and mysterious life were most discussed, he is quite forgotten. At times, indeed, some old lady will whisper to you at dinner, that a certain young man reminds her of Rupert Orange, only he is not so handsome; but she is one of those who keep the mere incidents of their past much more brightly polished than the important things of their present. The men who worshipped him, who copied his clothes, his walk, his mode of pronouncing words, and his manner of saying things, stare vaguely when he is mentioned. And the other day at a well-known club I was having some general talk with a man whose black hair is shot with white, when he exclaimed somewhat suddenly: "How little one hears about Rupert Orange now!" and then added: "I wonder what became of him?" As to the first part of this speech I kept my mouth resolutely shut; for how could I deny his saying, since I had lately seen a weed-covered grave with the early moss growing into the letters on the headstone? As to the second part, it is now my business to set forth the answer to that: and I think when the fire begins to blaze it will lighten certain recollections which have become dark. Of course, there are numberless people who never heard the story of Rupert Orange; but there are also crowds of men and women who followed his brilliant life with intense interest, while his shameful death will be in many a one's remembrance.

The knowledge of this case I got over a year ago; and I would have written then, had my hands been free. But there has recently died at Vienna the Countess de Volnay, whose notorious connection with Orange was at one time the subject of every man's bruit. Her I met two years since in Paris, where she was living like a work-woman. I learned that she had sold her house, and her goods she had given to the poor. She was still a remarkable woman, though her great beauty had faded, and despite a restless, terrified manner, which gave one the monstrous idea that she always felt the devil looking over her shoulder. Her hair was white as paper, and yet she was far from the age when women cease to grin in ball-rooms. A great fear seemed to have sprung to her face and been paralyzed there: a fear which could be detected in her shaking voice. It was from her that I learned certain primary facts of this narration; and she cried to me not to publish them till I heard of her death—as a man on the gallows sometimes asks the hangman not to adjust the noose too tight round his neck. I am altogether sure that what Orange himself told her, he never told any one else. I wish I had her running tongue instead of my slow pen, and then I would not be writing slovenly and clumsily, doubtless, for the relation; vainly, I am afraid, for the moral.

Now Rupert Orange lived with his aunt in New York till he was twenty-four years old, and when she died, leaving her entire estate to him, a furious contest arose over the will. Principal in the contest was Mrs. Annice, the wife of a discarded nephew; and she prosecuted the cause with the pertinacity and virulence which we often find in women of thirty. So good a pursuivant did she prove, that she and her husband leaped suddenly from indigence to great wealth: for the Court declared that the old lady had died lunatic; that she had been unduly influenced; and, that consequently her testament was void. But this decision, which raised them up, brought Rupert to the ground. There is no worse fall than the fall of a man from opulence to poverty; and Rupert, after his luxurious rearing, had to undergo this fall. Yet he had the vigour and confidence of the young. His little verses and sonnets had been praised when he was an amateur; now he undertook to make his pen a breadwinner—with the direst results. At first, nothing would do him but the great magazines; and from these, week after week, he received back his really clever articles, accompanied by cold refusals. Then for months he hung about the offices of every outcast paper, waiting for the editor. When at length the editor did come, he generally told Rupert that he had promised all his outlying work to some bar-room acquaintance. So push by push he was brought to his knees; and finally he dared not walk out till nightfall, for fear some of those who knew him in prosperity might witness his destitution.

One night early in December, about six o'clock, he left the mean flat-house on the west side of the city in which he occupied one room, and started (as they say in New York) "up town." The snow had frozen in lumps, and the gas lamps gleamed warmly on it for the man who had not seen a fire in months. When he reached Fifty-ninth Street, he turned east and skirted Central Park till he came to the Fifth Avenue. And here a sudden fancy seized him to walk this street, which shame and pride had kept him off since his downfall. He had not proceeded far, when he was stopped by an old man.

"Can you tell me, sir," says the old man, politely, "if this street runs on further than Central Park?"

"Oh, yes," answered Rupert, scraping at his throat; for he had not spoken to a soul for five days, and the phlegm had gathered. "It goes up a considerable distance from here."

"You'll forgive me asking you," went on the ancient. "I am only passing through the city, and I want to find out all I can."

"You're quite welcome," said Orange. "That," he added, pointing, "is St. Luke's Hospital."

They spoke a few more sentences, then as the stranger turned "down town," Rupert fell in with his walk. He did this partly because he was craving for fellowship; partly, too, from that feeling which certain men have—men who have never done anything for themselves in this world, and never will do anything—that distant relations, and even total strangers, are apt at any moment to fling fortunes into their hands. As they proceeded along the avenue, Orange turned to survey his companion. A shrewd wind was blowing, and it tossed the old gentleman's long beard over his shoulder, and ruffled the white hair under his soft hat. His clothes were plain, even shabby; and he had an odd trick of planting his feet on the ground without bending his knees, as though his legs were broomsticks. Orange thought, bitterly enough! how short a time had passed since the days when he would have taken poison as an alternative to walking down the Fifth Avenue with such an associate. Now, they were equal: or indeed the old man was the better off of the two: for if he wore impossible broad-toed boots, Orange had to stamp his feet to keep the cold from striking through his worn-out shoes. What cared he for the criticism of the smart, well-fed "Society" now, when numbers of that far greater society, of which he was one, were starving in garrets! As he thought these things a late afternoon reception began to pour out its crowds, and a young man and a girl, who had known Rupert in the days of his prosperity, came forth and glared with contempt at the two mean passengers. Not a muscle in Rupert's face quivered: he even afforded those two the tribute of a sneer.

When the pair of walkers reached Thirty-fourth Street they switched into Broadway. A silence had fallen between them, and it was in silence they paraded the thoroughfare. Here all was garish light and glare: carriages darted to and fro, restaurants were thronged, theatres ablaze, women smiling: everything told of a great city starting a night of pleasure. Besides the love of pleasure which was his main characteristic, Orange was distinctly gregarious; and the sight of all this joy, which he had once revelled in himself, struck like a knife into his hungry, lonely heart. At that moment he thought he would give his very soul to get some money.

"All these people seem happy," says the old man, suddenly.

"Yes," replied Orange. "They are happy enough!"

The old man caught the reply, and noticed the sour twang in it. He looked up quickly and saw that Rupert's eyes watered. "Why, man," he exclaimed, "I believe you're crying! or perhaps you're cold! Come in here, come right in to the Hoffman House!" he went on, tugging at Rupert's coat.

Rupert hesitated. The sensitiveness of one who had never taken a favour which he could not repay, held him back. But the desire for warmth and sympathy prevailed, so he entered. The usual crowd of loafers was about the bar, and those who composed it looked scoffingly at Orange's shiny overcoat and time-eaten trousers. Believe me, the man in rags is not half so pitiable as the poor creature who tries to maintain the appearance of a gentleman the man who inks scams by night which grow all white by day who keeps his fingers close pressed to his palm lest the rents in his glove be seen; who walks with his arm across his breast for fear his coat should fly open and proclaim its lack of buttons. Even the waiters looked disparagingly at Orange; and a waiter's jibes, or any flunkey's, are, perhaps, the sorest of all. But the old man, without noticing, sat down at a table and ordered a bottle of champagne. When the wine was brought, the two sat together some time in a muse. Then, of a sudden, the greybeard broke out.

"Wealth!" he cried, staring into Rupert's eyes, "wealth is the only thing worth striving for in this world! Your tub-philosophers may laugh at it, but they only laugh to keep away from themselves a cankering envy and desire which would be more bitter than their present lack. Let any man whom you call a genius arrive at this hotel to-night, and let a millionaire arrive at the same moment, and I'll bet you the millionaire gets the attention every time! A millionaire travels round the earth, and he gets respect everywhere he goes— why? Because he buys it. That's the way to get respect in the nineteenth century—buy it! Do the fine works of art which are sold each year go to the pauper student who worships them? No, sir, they go to the man who has the money) and who shells out the biggest price. I repeat, my young friend, that what's there" (and he slapped his pocket) "is what counts in the struggle of life."

"I agree with you," answered Orange, "that money counts for a great deal."

"A great deal repeated the other, scornfully, being now, perhaps, somewhat warmed with wine. A great deal! what have you to offer instead? Religion? Ministers are the parasites of rich men. Art? Go into the studio of any friend of yours to-morrow, and see whom he'll speak to first—you, or the man with a cheque in his hand. Why, if a poor man had the brains of Shakespeare, or our Emerson, and was mud-splashed by the carriage wheels of a wealthy woman, the only answer to his protests would be a policeman's 'move on!'"

"I know it! I know it!" cried Orange, in anguish. "I know it fifty times better than you do! I tell you I would sell my whole life now, for one year's perfect enjoyment of riches."

"Not one year," said the greybeard, leaning over the table and speaking so intensely that Rupert could hardly follow him. His old face had become ghastly and looked livid in contrast to the white hair. "Not one year, my boy, but five years! Think, only think, of the gloriousness of it all! This evening a despised pauper, to-morrow a rich man! Take courage, make up your mind to yield your life at the end of five years, and in return I will promise you, pledge you, that to-morrow morning you shall be in as sound a financial position as any man in New York."

Now it is strange that this outrageous proposal, made in thebar-room of an hotel situate in one of the most prosaic cities in the world, did not strike Rupert Orange as at all preposterous. Probably on account of his mystical, dreaming mind, he never took thought to doubt the speaker's sincereness, but at once fell to balancing the advantages and drawbacks of the scheme.

Five years! Before his young eyes they stretched out like fifty years. It did not occur to him (it rarely occurs to any young man) to hark back to the five preceding years and note how few and, swift were the strides which brought him over them to this very day he was living. Five years! They lay before him all silver with, sunshine, as he looked out from his present want and darkness. This was his point of view; and let us never forget this point of', view when we are passing judgment on him. No doubt, if the matter had been placed before a man of wealth, he would have denied it even momentary consideration: but the smell of cooking, is only disgusting to one who has dined; it is the vagrant who sniffs eagerly the air of the kitchen through the iron grating on, the street. For Rupert, at this moment, money meant all the world. He was a man who hated to face the bitter things of life and money included release from insolent creditors, from snubs and flouts, from a small, cold, dark room, and, chief of all! release from that horror which he saw drawing nearer and nearer: the gaol.

"There is one more word to be said," observed the old man, smoothly. "Leaving aside the contingency of your starving to death—which, by the way, I think very likely—there is a chance of your being run over by a cart when you leave this hotel. There is an even chance of your contracting some disease during the winter. How would you like to die in a pauper hospital, where the nurses sing as they close a dead man's eyes? Now, what I propose is, that you shall be free from any physical pain for five years."

"If I should accept," said Orange, swirling the wine round in his glass till it creamed and foamed, "I'd desire some slight ills to take the very sweetness out of life." Probably he meant, for fear that when his time came he should hate to die.

He thought again. He was like to a man who arrives suddenly at a mountain village on the feast of the Blessed Sacrament, and loitering in the street with his eyes enchanted by the tawdry decorations and festoons of the houses, forgets to look beyond at the awful mountain standing against the sky, with menacing thunder clouds about its breast. Before Orange's mind a gay and tempting pageant defiled. He thought of the travels he would be able to make, of luxurious palaces, of exquisite banquets, of priceless wines, of laughing, rapturous women. He thought, too, for he was far from being a merely sensuous man, of the first editions he could buy, of the rare gems, of dainty bindings. Sweetest of all were the thoughts, that he would be at his ease to do the best work that it was in him to do, and that he would be powerful enough to wreak his vengeance on his enemies very slowly, inch by inch. With that, like the crack of a rifle shot, came the thought of Mrs. Annice.

He sprang to his feet. "Listen!" he cried, in such a voice that the idlers at the bar turned round for a moment; but observing that no row was in progress to divert them, they fell once more to their drinking. "Listen!" cried Rupert Orange again, gripping the side of the table with one hand and pointing a shaking finger at the old man. "There is one woman alive in this city to-night who has brought me to the degradation which you witness now. She flung me to the ground, she covered me with dust, she crushed me beneath her merciless heel! Give her to me that I may lower her pride! let me see her as abject and despised as the poorest trull that walks the streets, and I swear by God Most High to make the bargain!"

The old man grasped Rupert's cold hand, and pressed it between his own feverishly hot palms. "It is an unusual taste," he murmured, glancing into Rupert's eyes, and smiling faintly.

Chapter II

Orange started, "up town" with a song in his heart. Curiously enough, he had not the slightest doubt about the genuineness of the contract, nor had he the least sorrow for what he had done. It mattered little about snubs and side looks to-night: to-morrow men and women would joyfully begin pawing him and fawning. So happy was he, his blood danced through his veins so merrily, that he ran for three or four blocks; and once he laughed a loud laugh, which caused a policeman to menace him with a club. But this Only brought him more merriment; to-morrow, if he liked, he could laugh from Central Park to Madison Square without molestation.

When he reached the mean flat-house on the west side, there was, as usual, no light in the entrance, and he saw a postman groping among the bells.

"Say, young feller!" began the postman, "do you know if any one by the name of Orange is kickin' around this blamed house?"

"I am he," said Rupert Orange, and held out his hand for the letter.

"Yes, you are answered," said the postman, derisively. "Now then, come off the roof and shew us the bell."

Rupert indicated the place, and, as soon as the postman had dropped the letter, he whipped out his key, and to the postman's surprise unlocked the box and put the letter in his pocket.

"Well! you see my business is to deliver letters, not to give them away," said the postman, making an official distinction. "When you said you was the man, how was I to know you wasn't givin' me a steer?"

"Oh, that's all right!" replied Rupert. "Good night, my friend."

He went upstairs to his freezing little room, and sat down to think. He would not open the letter yet: his mind was too crowded to admit any new emotion. So for two hours he remained dreaming brilliant and fantastic dreams. Then he tore open the envelope. He was so poor that the gas had been turned off from his room, but by the light of a match he read a communication from Messrs. Daroll and Kettel, the lawyers, setting forth that a distant relative of his had recently died in a town in one of the Southern States, and had left him a fortune of nearly a million dollars. But Rupert knew that this million dollars was only nominal, that money would remain with him as long as he could call life his own.

The charwoman who came into his room next morning, found him asleep in the chair, with the letter open on his knee, and a smile lighting his face. But he was only a pauper, in arrears for his rent, so she struck him smartly between the shoulders with her broom.

"I believe I've been asleep," said Rupert, starting and rubbing his eyes. The woman looked at him sourly, thinking that he would have to take his next sleep in one of the parks. She began to sweep the dust in his direction till he coughed violently.

"You have been very good to me since I've been here, Mrs. Spill," Rupert continued; and, I think, without irony: he had not much idea of irony. He took from his pocket the last five-dollar bill he had in the world and gave it to her. "Please take that for your trouble."

The woman stared at him, as she would have stared had he cut his throat before her eyes. But Orange clapped on his hat and rushed out. He had not even the five cents necessary to travel down town in a horse-car, so he walked the distance to the office of Messrs. Daroll and Kettel, in Pine Street. He approached a fat clerk (who, decked as he was with doubtful jewellery, looked as if he were honouring the office by being in it at all), and asked if Mr. Kettel was within. Now it is something worthy of note, that I have often called on men occupied with difficult texts; or painting pictures; or writing novels; and each one had been able to let go his work at once: while, on the other hand, it is your part to await the pleasure of a clerk, till he has finished his enthralling occupation. True to his breed, the fat man kept Rupert standing before him for about three minutes, till he had elaborately finished a copy of a bill of details; and then looking up, and seeing only a shabby fellow, he asked sharply:—

"Eh? What do you say?"

Rupert repeated his question.

"Yes, I guess he's in, but this is his busy day. You just sit right down there, young man, and he'll see you when he gets good and ready."

The hard knocks which Rupert had received in his contest with the world had taken out of him the self-assertion that goes with wealth: so he sat for half an hour, knowing well, meanwhile, that his clothes were a cause for laughter to the underbred and badly trained clerks. At length he somewhat timidly went over to the desk again.

Perhaps if you would be kind enough to take my name into Mr. Kettel—-"

"Oh, look here, make me tired!" exclaimed the fat clerk, irritably. "Didn't I tell you that he you was busy? Now, I don't want to see you monkeying round this desk any more! If you don't want to wait, why the walking's pretty good!——This young man says he wants to see you," he added, as Mr. Kettel came out of his private room.

"Well, sir, what do you want to-day?" asked Mr. Kettel, with that most offensive tone and air which some misguided men imagine will impress the spectator as a manner for the man of great affairs. "You had better call round some other time; we're not able to attend—-" he was going on, when he happened to look narrowly into Rupert's face, and his manner changed in a second. "Why, my dear boy, how are you! it's so long since I've seen you, that I didn't know at first. And, how you've changed!" he went on, and could not help a glance at Rupert's shabby dress; for he was quite ignoble. Then this remark seeming of questionable taste even to him, he cried heartily: "But come into my private room, and we can have a good long chat!" And in he went, with Rupert at his heels, leaving the fat clerk at gaze.

In a week Rupert was once more dawdling about clubs, and attending those social functions which go to make up what is called a Season. Above all, he was listening to an appalling variety of apologetic lies. To the average man who said: "We didn't know when on earth you were coming back from Europe, my dear fellow; how did you like it over there?" he could answer with a grave face; but the women were different. One particular afternoon he was at a reception, when he heard a lady near him remark in clear accents to her friend: "You can't think how we missed that dear Mr. Orange while he was away in Africa!" and this struck Rupert as so grotesque that he apparently laughed. Amid this social intercourse, however, he avoided sedulously a meeting with Mrs. Annice; he had decided not to see her for a while. Indeed, it was not till an evening late in February, after dinner, that he took a cab to her house near Washington Square. He found her at home, and had not waited a minute before she came into the room. She was a tall woman, and wonderfully handsome by gaslight; but she had that tiresome habit, which many women have, of talking intensely—in italics, as it were: a habit found generally in women ill brought up-women without control of their feelings, or command of the expression of them.

"My dear, dear Rupert, how glad I am to see you," she exclaimed, throwing a white fluffy cloak off her bare shoulders, and holding out both hands as she glided towards him. "It is so long, that I really thought we were never going to see you again. But I am so glad. And how very fortunate that legacy was for you—just when I suppose you were working fearfully hard. I was quite delighted when I heard of it, and my husband too. He would have been so pleased to have seen you, but he is dining out to-night."

There was a tone of too much hypocrisy about all this, and Rupert made full allowance for it. He chatted in his easy way about his good fortune, and recited some details.

"I suppose there is not the slightest possibility of a flaw in the will?" says Mrs. Annice, regarding him keenly. The lines round her mouth had become hard, but she kept on smiling: she had some traits like Macbeth's wife.

Orange laughed his bright, merry laugh which so few could resist. "Oh no, I think it's all right this time," he said, and looked at her steadfastly with his fine eyes.

Mrs. Annice suddenly flushed, and then shuddered. Her heart began to throb, her head to whirl. What was the matter with her? What was this cursed sensation which was mastering her? She, with her self-poise, her deliberateness, her calculation, was, in the flash of an eye, brought to feel towards this man, whom but a moment ago she had hated more than any one in the world, as she had never felt towards man before. It was not love, this wretched thraldom, it was not even admiration; it was a wild desire to abnegate herself, annihilate herself, in this man's personality; to become his bond-woman, the slave of his controlling will. She drove the nails into her palms, and crushed her lips between her teeth, as she rose to her feet and made one desperate try for victory.

"I was just going to the opera when you came in, Rupert," she said; "won't you come in my box?"—and her voice had so changed, there was such a note of tenderness and desire in it, that it seemed as if she had exposed her soul. But even in her disorganised state she was conscious that there would be a certain distinction in appearing at the opera with the re-edified Rupert Orange.

Rupert murmured something about the opera being such a bore, and at that moment the footman announced the carriage.

"Won't you come?" asked Mrs. Annice, standing with her white hand resting on the back of a chair.

"I think not," answered Rupert, with a smile.

She dismissed the carriage. As soon as the servant had gone she tried to make some trivial remark, and, half turning, looked at Orange, who rose. For an instant those two stood gazing into each other's eyes with God knows what hell in their hearts, and then, with a little cry, that was half a sob, she flung her arms about his neck, and pressed her kisses on his lips.

Chapter III

Yesterday afternoon I took from amongst my books a novel of Rupert Orange, and as I turned over the leaves, I fell to pondering how difficult it is to obtain any of his works to-day, while but a few years ago all the world was reading them; and to lose myself in amaze at our former rapturous and enthusiastic admiration of his literary art, his wit, his pathos. For in truth his art is a very tawdry art to my present liking; his wit is rather stale, his pathos a little vulgar. And the charm has likewise gone out of his poetry: even his Chaunt of the Storm-Witch, which we were used to think so melodious and sonorous, now fails to please. To explain the precise effect which his poetry has upon me now, I am forced to resort to a somewhat unhappy figure; I am forced to say that his poetry has an effect on me like sifted ashes! I cannot in the least explain this figure; and if it fails to convey any idea to the reader, I am afraid the failure must be set down to my clumsy writing. And yet what praise we all bestowed on these works of Rupert Orange! How eagerly we watched for them to appear; how we prized them; with what zeal we studied the newspapers for details of his interesting and successful life!

A particular account of that brilliant and successful life it would ill become me to chronicle, even if I were so minded: it was with no purpose of relating his social and literary triumphs, his continual victories during five years in the two fields he had chosen to conquer, that I started to write. But in dwelling on his life, we must not forget to take account of these triumphs. They were very rare, very proud, very precious triumphs, both in Europe and in the United States; triumphs that few men ever enjoy; triumphs which were potent enough to deaden the pallid thought of the curious limits of his life, except on three sombre occasions.

It was on the first night of a new opera at Covent Garden, Orange was in a box with a notable company, and was on the point of leaning over to whisper something amusing to the beautiful Countess of Heston, when of a sudden he shot white, and the smile left his face as if he had received a blow. On the stage a chorus had commenced in a very low tone of passionate entreaty; by degrees it swelled louder and louder, till it burst forth into a tremendous agonised prayer for pity and pardon. As Orange listened, such a dreary sense of the littleness of life, such an awful fear of death, sang through his brain, that he grew sick, and shivered in a cold sweat.

"Why, I'm afraid Mr. Orange is ill exclaimed the Countess.

"No, no!" muttered Orange, groping for his hat. "Only a little faint; want some air!—I tell you I want some air!" he broke out in a voice that was like a frightened cry, as he fumbled with the door of the box.

A certain man with a kind heart followed him into the foyer.

"Can I do anything for you, old chap?"

"Yes; in the name of God leave me alone!" replied Orange and he said it in such a tone, and with a face so frightfully contorted, that those standing about fell back feeling queer, and the questioner returned to the box very gravely, and thought on his soul for the rest of the evening.

But Orange rushed out, and he hailed a hansom, and he drove till the cabman refused to drive any more; and then he walked; and it was not till he found himself on Putney Heath in his evening dress, at half-past twelve the next day, that the devil left him.

About two years after this occurrence he was wandering one Sunday evening in Chelsea, and hearing a church bell ring for the usual service, he decided to enter. As he sat waiting a little girl of four or five, with her mother, came in and sat by him: and Rupert talked to the child in his quaint, winning way, and so won her, that when the service began she continued to cling to his hand. After a while the sermon commenced, and the preacher, taking for his text the words: "And he died," from the fifth chapter of Genesis, tried to set forth the suddenness and unwelcomeness of death, even to the long-lived patriarchs, and its increased suddenness and unwelcomeness to most of us. The sermon I suppose, was dull and commonplace enough, but if the speaker had verily seen into the mind of one of his listeners, the effect could not have been more disastrous. Orange waited till the torture became unbearable, till he could actually feel the horrid, stifling weight of earth pressing him down in his coffin, and keeping him there for ages and ages: then with a heavy groan he started up, and rushed forth with such vehemence, that he knocked down and trampled on the little girl, in his haste to get out of sight of the white faces of people scared at his face, and the child's sad cry was borne to him out in the dark street.

The third occasion on which this sense of despair and loss oppressed him, was at a time when he was near a rugged coast. One stormy day he rode to a certain promontory, and came sudenly in sight of the great sea. As he stood watching a lonely gull, that strained, and swooped, and dipped in the surge, while the rain drizzled, and the wind whined through the long grass, the futility of his life stung him, and he hid his face in his horse's mane and wept.

But sorest of all was the thought that he might really have won a certain fame, an easy fortune, without taking on his back the fardel which, as the months went by, became so heavy. He knew that he had done some work which would have surely gained him distinction, had he but waited. Why did you not have patience his outraged spirit and maimed life seemed to moan; a little more patience!

I must not let you think, however, that he was unhappy. In every detail the promise of the old man was punctiliously carried out. The very maladies which Orange had desired, were twisted to his advantage. Thus, when he was laid up with a sprained ankle at an hotel at Aix-les-Bains, he formed his notorious connection with Gabrielle de Volnay. It was when he was kept for a day in the house by a cold that he wrote his little comedy, Her Ladyship's Dinner—a comedy which at one time, we were all so forward to praise. And on the night upon which his cab was overturned in the Sixth Avenue, New York, and he was badly cut about the head, did he not recognise in the drunken prostitute who cursed him, the erstwhile brilliant Mrs. Annice? Did he not forget his pain in the exquisite knowledge that her curses were of no avail, and flout her jeeringly, brutally? Nay! when an epidemic disease broke out in a certain part of the Riviera, and the foreign population presently fled, he used his immunity from death to hold his ground and tend the sick, and so gave cause to the newspapers to proclaim the courage and devotion of Mr. Orange. And all these fortunate incidents were suddenly brought to completeness by one singular event.

It was on a winter morning, about three o'clock, that he found himself in the district of Kilburn, and noticed a crimson stain on the sky. More from indolence than from anything else he went towards the fire; but when he came in sight of it, he was startled by a somewhat strange thing. For there at a window high up in the blazing house, stood a woman with a baby in her arms, who had clearly been left to a hideous fate on account of the fierceness of the flames. With an abrupt gesture Orange flung off his cloak.

"Where can I find the chief?" he asked a man standing near, "because I'm going up?"

The fellow turned, and seeing Rupert in his evening suit, laughed derisively.

"I say Bill!" he sings out to his mate, "this 'ere bloke says as how he's goin' up!" and the other's scoffing reply struck Rupert's ears as he pushed through the crowd.

By a letter which he carried with him, or some such authority, Orange gained his request; and the next thing that the people saw was a ladder rigged, and the figure of a man ascending through clouds of smoke. Higher and higher he went, while the flames lick and sizzled around him and scared his flesh: higher and higher till he had almost reached the window, and a wild cheer burst from the crowd for such a deed of heroism. But at that moment a long tongue of flame leaped into the sky, the building tottered and then crashed down, and Orange was safely caught by some strong arms, while the woman and child met death within the ruins. Of course this affair was noised abroad the next day; for some weeks Orange, with his hand in a sling, was a picturesque figure in several London drawing-rooms.

Now, which one of us shall say that Orange, with the tested knowledge of his exemption from death, and strong in that knowledge, deliberately did this heroic act to improve his fame, to exalt his honour? I have stated before that we must be cautious in passing judgment on him, and I must again insist on this caution. As for myself, I should be sorry to think that there is no beautiful merciful Spirit to note an unselfish impulse, which took no thought of glory or advertisement, and count it to the man for honesty.

But the time ran, and the years sped, until was come the last month of that fifth year, which meant the end of years for Orange. When in the days of his happiness and strength, he had dwelt on this time at all, he had planned to seek out, on the last day of the year, some mountain crag in Switzerland, and there meet death, coming in the train of the rising sun, with calm and steady eyes. Alas! now to his anguish he felt a desire, which was stronger than his will, tearing at his heart to visit once more the scene of his hardships, to look again on the place where his bargain was concluded. I make certain, from a letter of his which I have seen, that in taking passage for New York, Rupert had no idea of turning aside his doom. The Cambria, on which he sailed, was due to arrive at New York a full week before the end of the year; but she encountered baffling winds and seas, and it was not till the evening of the thirty-first of December that she sighted the light on Fire Island.

As the steamer went at speed towards Sandy Hook, Orange stood alone on the deck, watching the smoke from her funnel rolling seaward: of a sudden he saw rise out of the cloud, the presentment, grim and menacing, of God the Father.

Chapter IV

As the Cambria moved up towards the city, on the morning of New Year's Day, a certain frenzy which was half insane, and a fierce loathing of familiar sights—Castle Garden, the spire of Trinity Church—took hold of Orange. He passionately cursed himself for not staying in Europe; he cursed the hour he was born; he cursed, above all! the hour in which he had made that fatal bargain. As soon as the vessel was made fast to the dock, he hastened ashore; and leaving his servant to look after his luggage, he sprang into a hack, and directed the driver to go "up town."

"Where to, boss?" inquired the man, looking at him curiously.

"The Hoffman House," replied Orange, before he thought. Then he cursed himself again, but he did not change the order.

I have said that the driver looked at Orange curiously; and in truth he was a strange sight. All the dignity of his demeanour was gone: his eyes were bloodshot, and his complexion a dirty yellow: he was unshorn, his tic was loose, and his collar open. His terror grew as he passed along the well-known streets: he screamed out hateful, obscene things, rolling about in the vehicle, while moam came from his mouth; and as he arrived at the hotel, in his distraction he drove his hand through the window glass, which cut him into the bone.

"An accident," he panted hoarsely to the porter who opened the door: "a slight accident! God damn you!" he yelled, "can't you see it was an accident?" and he went up the hall to the office, leaving behind him a trail of blood. The clerk at the desk, seeing his disorder, was on the point of refusing him a room; but when Orange wrote his name in the visitor's book, he smirked, and ordered the best set of apartments in the house to be made ready. To these apartments Orange retired, and sat all day in a sort of dull horror. For a sudden death he had in a measure prepared himself: he had made his bargain, he had bought his freedom from the cares which are the burthen of all men and he knew that he must pay the debt: but for some uncertain, treacherous calamity he had not prepared. He was not fool enough to dream that the one to whom the debt was owed would relent: but before his creditor's method of exacting payment he was at a stand. He thought and thought, rubbing his face in his hands, till his head was near bursting: in a sudden spasm he fell off the chair to the floor; and that night he was lying stricken by typhoid fever.

And for weeks he lay with a fiery forehead and blazing eyes, finding the lightest covering too heavy and ice too hot. Even when the known disease seemed to have been subdued, certain strange complications arose which puzzled the physicians: amongst these a painful vomiting which racked the man's frame and left an exhaustion akin to death, and a curious loathly decay of the flesh. This last was so venomous an evil, that one of the nurses having touched the sick man in her ministrations, and neglected to immediately purify herself, within a few hours incontinently deceased. After a while, to assist these enemies of Orange, there came pneumonia. It would seem as though he were experiencing all the maladies from which he had been free during the past five years; for besides his corporal ills he had become lunatic, and he was raving. Those who tended him, used as they were to outrageous scenes, shuddered and held each other's hands when they heard him shriek his curses, and realised his abject fear of death. At times, too, they would hear him weeping softly, and whispering the broken little prayers he had learned in childhood: praying God to save him in this dark hour from the wiles of the devil.

At length, one evening towards the end of March, the mental clearness of Orange somewhat revived, and he felt himself compelled to get up and put on his clothes. The nurse, thinking that the patient was resting quietly, and fearing the shine of the lamp might distress him, had turned it low and gone away for a little: so it was without interruption, although reeling from giddiness, and scorched with fever, that Rupert groped about till he found some garments, and his evening suit. Clad in these, and throwing a cloak over his shoulders, he went downstairs. Those whom he met, that recognised him, looked at him wonderingly and with a vague dread; but he appeared to have his understanding as well as they, and so he passed through the hall without being stopped; and going into the bar, he called for brandy. The bar-tender, to whom he was known, exclaimed in astonishment; but he got no reply from Orange, who, pouring himself out a large quantity of the fiery liquor found it colder than the coldest iced water in his burning frame. When he had taken the brandy, he went into the street. It was a bleak seasonable night, and a bitter frost-rain was falling: but Orange went through it, as if the bitter weather was a not unwelcome coolness, although he shuddered in an ague-fit. As he stood on the corner of Twenty-third Street, his cloak thrown open, the sleet sowing down on his shirt, and the slush which covered his ankles soaking through his thin shoes, a member of his club came by and spoke to him.

"Why, good God! Orange, you don't mean to say you're out on a night like this! You must be much better—eh?" he broke off, for Orange had given him a grey look, with eyes in which there was no speculation; and the man hurried away scared and rather aghast. "These poet chaps are always queer fishes," he muttered uneasily, as he turned into the Fifth Avenue Hotel.

Of the events of terror and horror which happened on that awful night, when a human soul was paying the price of an astonishing violation of the order of the universe, no man shall ever tell. Blurred, hideous, and enormous visions of dives, of hells where the worst scum of the town consorted, of a man who spat on him, of a woman who struck him across the face with her umbrella, calling him the foulest of names—visions such as these, and more hateful than these, presented themselves to Orange, when he found himself, at three o'clock in the morning, standing under a lamp-post in that strange district of New York called "The Village."

The rain had given way to a steady fall of snow: and as he stood there, a squalid harlot, an outcast amongst outcasts, approached, and solicited him in the usual manner.

"Come along—do!" she said, shivering: "We can get a drink at my place."

Receiving no answer, she peered into his face, and gave a cry of loathing and fear.

"Oh, look here!" she said, roughly, coughing down her disgust: "You've been drinking too much, and you've got a load. Come ahead with me and you can have a good sleep."

At that word Orange turned, and gazed at her with a vacant, dreary, silly smile. He raised his hand, and when she shrank away—"Are you afraid of me?" he said, not coarsely, but quietly, even gently, like a man talking in his sleep. Then they went on together, till they came to a dilapidated house close by the river. They entered, and turned into a dirty room lit by a flaring jet of gas.

"Now, dear; let's have some money," says the woman, "and I'll get you a nice drink."

Still no answer from Orange: only that same vacant smile, which was beginning to be horrible.

"Give me some money: do you hear!" cried the woman stridently. Then she seized him, and went through his pockets in an accustomed style, and found three cents.

"What the hell do you mean by coming here with only this!" bellowed the woman, holding out the mean coins to Orange. She struck him; but she was very frightened, and went to the stairs.

"Say! Tom—Tommy," she called; "you'd better come down and put this loafer out!"

A great hulking man came down the stairs, and gazed for an instant at Rupert—standing under the gas-jet, with the woman plucking the studs from his shirt. For an instant the man stood, feeling sick and in a sweat; and then, by a great effort, he approached Orange, and seized him by the collar.

"Here, out you go!" he said. "We don't want none of your sort around here!" The man dragged Orange to the street door, and gave the wretch such a powerful shove, that he fell on the pavement, and rolled into the gutter.

And later in the morning, one who passed by the way found him there: dead before the squalid harlot's door.

The Business of Madame Jahn

How we all stared, how frightened we all were, how we passed opinions, on that morning when Gustave Herbout was found swinging by the neck from the ceiling of his bedroom. The whole Faubourg, even the ancient folk who had not felt a street under them for years, turned out and stood gaping at the house with amazement and loud conjecture. For why should Gustave Herbout, of all men, take to the rope? Only last week he had inherited all the money of his aunt, Madame Jahn, together with her house and the shop with the five assistants, and life looked fair enough for him. No; clearly it was not wise of Gustave to hang himself!

Besides, his aunt's death had happened at a time when Gustave was in sore straits for money. To be sure, he had his salary from the bank in which he worked; but what is a mere salary to one who (like Gustave) threw off the clerkly habit when working hours were over to assume the dress and lounge of the accustomed boulevardier: while he would relate to obsequious friends vague but satisfactory stories of a Russian Prince who was his uncle, and of an extremely rich English lady to whose death he looked forward with hope. Alas! with a clerk's salary one cannot make much of a figure in Paris. It took all of that, and more, to maintain the renown he had gained among his acquaintance of having to his own a certain little lady with yellow hair who danced divinely. So he was forced to depend on the presents which Madame Jahn gave him from time to time; and for those presents he had to pay his aunt a most sedulous and irksome attention. At times, when he was almost sick from his craving for the boulevard, the café, the theatre, he would have to repair as the day grew to an end, to our Faubourg, and the house behind the shop, where he would sit to an old-fashioned supper with his aunt, and listen With a sort of dull impatience while she asked him when he had last been at Confession, and told him long dreary stories of his dead father and mother. Punctually at nine o'clock the deaf servant, who was the only person besides Madame Jahn that lived in the house, would let in the fat old priest, who came for his game of dominoes, and betake herself to bed. Then the dominoes would begin, and with them the old man's prattle which Gustave knew so well: about his daily work, about the uselessness of all things here on earth, and the happiness and glory of the Kingdom of Heaven; and, of course, our boulevardier noticed, with the usual cheap sneer of the modern, that whilst the priest talked of the Kingdom of Heaven he yet showed the greatest anxiety if he had symptoms of a cold, or any other petty malady. However, Gustave would sit there with a hypocrite's grin and inwardly raging, till the clock chimed eleven. At that hour Madame Jahn would rise, and, if she was pleased with her nephew, would go over to her writing-desk and give him, with a rather pretty air of concealment from the priest, perhaps fifty or a hundred francs. Whereupon Gustave would bid her a manifestly affectionate good-night! and depart in the company of the priest. As soon as he could get rid of the priest, he would hasten to his favourite cafés, to discover that all the people worth seeing had long since grown tired of waiting and had departed on their own affairs. The money, indeed, was a kind of consolation; but then there were nights when he did not get a sou. Ah! they amuse themselves in Paris, but not in this way—this is not amusing.

One cannot live a proper life upon a salary and an occasional gift of fifty or a hundred francs. And it is not entertaining to tell men that your uncle, the Prince at Moscow, is in a sorry case, and even now lies a-dying, or that the rich English lady is in the grip of a vile consumption and is momently expected to succumb, if these men only shove up their shoulders, wink at one another, and continue to present their bills. Further, the little Mademoiselle with yellow hair had lately shown signs of a very pretty temper, because her usual flowers and bon-bons were not apparent. So, since things were come to this dismal pass, Gustave fell to attending the race-meetings at Chantilly. During the first week Gustave won largely, for that is sometimes the way with ignorant men: during that week, too, the little Mademoiselle was charming, for she had her bouquets and boxes of bon-bons. But the next week Gustave lost heavily, for that is also very often the way with ignorant men: and he was thrown into the blackest despair, when one night at a place where he used to sup, Mademoiselle took the arm of a great fellow whom he much suspected to be a German, and tossed him a scornful nod as she went off.

On the evening after this happened, he was standing between five and six o'clock, in the Place de la Madeleine, blowing on his fingers and trying to plan his next move, when he heard his name called by a familiar voice, and turned to face his aunt's adviser, the priest.

"Ah, Gustave, my friend, I have just been to see a colleague of mine here!" cried the old man, pointing to the great church. "And are you going to your good aunt to-night?" he added, with a look at Gustave's neat dress.

Gustave was in a flame that the priest should have detected him in his gay clothes, for he always made a point of appearing at Madame Jahn's clad staidly in black; but he answered pleasantly enough:

"No, my Father, I'm afraid I can't to-night. You see I'm a little behind with my office work, and I have to stay at home and catch up."

"Well, well said the priest, with half a sigh, I suppose young men will always be the same. I myself can only be with her till nine o'clock to-night because I must see a sick parishioner. But let me give you one bit of advice, my friend," he went on, taking hold of a button on Gustave's coat: "Don't neglect your aunt; for, mark my words, one day everything of Madame Jahn's will be yours!" And the omnibus he was waiting for happening to swing by at that moment, he departed without another word.

Gustave strolled along the Boulevard des Capucines in a study. Yes; it was certain that the house, and the shop with the five assistants, would one day be his; for the priest knew all his aunt's affairs. But how soon would they be his? Madame Jahn was now hardly sixty; her mother had lived to be ninety; when she was ninety he would be——And meanwhile, what about the numerous bills, what (above all!) about the little lady with yellow hair? He paused and struck his heel on the pavement with such force, that two men passing nudged one another and smiled. Then he made certain purchases, and set about wasting his time till nine o'clock.

It is curious to consider, that although when he started out at nine o'clock, Gustave was perfectly clear as to what he meant to do, yet he was chiefly troubled by the fear that the priest had told his aunt about his fine clothes. But when he had passed through the deserted Faubourg, and had come to the house behind the shop, he found his aunt only very pleased to see him, and a little surprised. So he sat with her, and listened to her gentle, homely stories, and told lies about himself and his manner of life, till the clock struck eleven. Then he rose, and Madame Jahn rose too and went to her writing-desk and opened a small drawer.

"You have been very kind to a lonely old woman to-night, my Gustave," said Madame Jahn, smiling.

"How sweet of you to say that, dearest aunt!" replied Gustave. He went over and passed his arm caressingly across her shoulders, and stabbed her in the heart.

For a full five minutes after the murder he stood still; as men often do in a great crisis when they know that any movement means decisive action. Then he started, laid hold of his hat, and made for the door. But there the stinging knowledge of his crime came to him for the first time; and he turned back into the room. Madame Jahn's bedroom candle was on a table: he lit it, and passed through a door which led from the house into the shop. Crouching below the counters covered with white sheets, lest a streak of light on the windows might attract the observation of some passenger, he proceeded to a side entrance to the shop, unbarred and unlocked the door and put the key in his pocket. Then, in the same crouching way, he returned to the room, and started to ransack the small drawer. The notes he scattered about the floor; but two small bags of coin went into his coat. Then he took the candle and dropped some wax on the face and hands and dress of the corpse; he spilt wax, too, over the carpet, and then he broke the candle and ground it under his foot. He even tore with long nervous fingers at the dead woman's bodice until her breasts lay exposed; and plucked out a handful of her hair and threw it on the floor to stick to the wax. When all these things had been accomplished he went to the house door and listened. The Faubourg is always very quiet about twelve o'clock, and a single footstep falls on the night with a great sound. He could not hear the least noise; so he darted out and ran lightly until he came to a turning. There he fell into a sauntering walk, lit a cigarette, and, hailing a passing fiacre, directed the man to drive to the Pont Saint-Michel. At the bridge he alighted, and noting that he was not eyed, he threw the key of the shop into the river. Then assuming the swagger and assurance of a half-drunken man, he marched up the Boulevard and entered the Café d'Harcourt.

The place was filled with the usual crowd of men and women of the Quartier Latin. Gustave looked round, and observing a young student with a flushed face who was talking eagerly about the rights of man, he sat down by him. It was his part to act quickly so before the student had quite finished a sentence for his car, the murderer gave him the lie. The student, however, was not so ready for a fight as Gustave had supposed; and when he began to argue again, Gustave seized a glass full of brandy and water and threw the stuff in his face. Then indeed there was a row, till the gendarmes interfered, and haled Gustave to the station. At the police-station he bitterly lamented his misdeed, which he attributed to an extra glass of absinthe, and he begged the authorities to carry word of his plight to his good aunt, Madame Jahn, in our Faubourg. So to the house behind the shop they went, and there they found her—sitting with her breasts hanging out, her poor head clotted with blood, and a knife in her heart.

The next morning, Gustave was set free. A man and a woman, two of the five assistants in the shop, had been charged with the murder. The woman had been severely reprimanded by Madame Jahn on the day before, and the man was known to be the girl's paramour. It was the duty of the man to close at night all the entrances into the shop, save the main entrance, which was closed by Madame Jahn and her deaf servant; and the police had formed a theory (worked out with the amazing zeal and skill which cause the Paris police so often to overreach themselves!) that the man had failed to bolt one of the side doors, and had, by his subtilty, got possession of the key whereby he and his accomplice re-entered the place about midnight. Working on this theory, the police had woven a web round the two unfortunates with threads of steel; and there was little doubt that both of them would stretch their necks under the guillotine, with full consent of Press and public. At least, this was Gustave's opinion; and Gustave's opinion now went for a great deal in the Faubourg. Of course there were a few who murmured that it was a good thing poor Madame Jahn had not lived to see her nephew arrested for a drunken brawler; but with full remembrance of who owned the house and shop we were most of us inclined to say, after the priest: That if the brave Gustave had been with

48

his aunt, the shocking affair could never have occurred. And, indeed, what had we more inspiring than the inconsolable grief he showed? Why! on the day of the funeral, when he heard the earth clatter down on the coffin-lid in Père la Chaise, he even swooned to the ground, and had to be carried out in the midst of the mourners. "Oh, yes," (quoth the gossips), "Gustave Herbout loved his aunt passing well!"

On the night after the funeral, Gustave was sitting alone before the fire in Madame Jahn's room, smoking and making his plans. He thought, that when all this wretched mock grief and pretence of decorum was over, he would again visit the cafés which he greatly savoured, and the little Mademoiselle with yellow hair would once more smile on him delicious smiles with a gleaming regard. Thus he was thinking when the clock on the mantel-piece tinkled eleven; and at that moment a very singular thing happened. The door was suddenly opened: a girl came in, and walked straight over to the writing-desk, pulled out the small drawer, and then sat staring at the man by the fire. She was distinctly beautiful; although there was a certain old-fashionedness in her peculiar silken dress, and the manner of wearing her hair. Not once did it occur to Gustave, as he gazed in terror, that he was gazing on a mortal woman: the doors were too well bolted to allow anyone from outside to enter, and besides, there was a strange baffling familiarity in the face and mien of the intruder. It might have been an hour as he sat there; and then, the silence becoming too horrible, by a supreme effort of his wonderful courage he rushed out of the room and up-stairs to get his hat. There in his murdered aunt's bedroom,—there, smiling at him from the wall—was a vivid presentment of the dread vision that sat below: a portrait of Madame Jahn as a girl. He fled into the street, and walked, perhaps two miles, before he thought at all. But when he did think, he found that he was drawn against his will back to the house to see if It was still there: just as the police here believe a murderer is drawn to the Morgue to view the body of his victim. Yes; the girl was there still, with her great reproachless eyes; and throughout that solemn night Gustave, haggard and mute, sat glaring at her. Towards dawn he fell into an uneasy doze; and when he awoke with a scream, he found that the girl was gone.

At noon the next day Gustave, heartened by several glasses of brandy, and cheered by the sunshine in the Champs-Elysées, endeavoured to make light of the affair. He would gladly have arranged not to go back to the house: but then people would talk so much, and he could not afford to lose any custom out of the shop. Moreover, the whole matter was only an hallucination—the effect of jaded nerves. He dined well, and went to see a musical comedy; and so contrived, that he did not return to the house until after two o'clock. There was someone waiting for him, sitting at the desk with the small drawer open; not the girl of last night, but a somewhat older woman—and the same reproachless eyes. So great was the fascination of those eyes, that, although he left the house at once with an iron resolution not to go back, he found himself drawn under them again, and he sat through the night as he had sat through the night before, sobbing and stupidly glaring. And all day long he crouched by the fire shuddering; and all the night till eleven o'clock; and then a figure of his aunt came to him again, but always a little older and more withered. And this went on for five days; the figure that sat with him becoming older and older as the days ran, till on the sixth night he gazed through the hours at his aunt as she was on the night he killed her. On these nights he was used sometimes to start up and make for the street, swearing never to return; but always he would be dragged back to the eyes. The policemen came to know him from these night walks, and people began to notice his bad looks: these could not spring from grief, folk said, and so they thought he was leading a wild life.

On the seventh night there was a delay of about five minutes after the clock had rung eleven, before the door opened. And then—then, merciful God! The body of a woman in grave-clothes came into the room, as if borne by unseen men, and lay in the air across the writing-desk, while the small drawer flew open of its own accord. Yes; there was the shroud and the brown scapular, the prim white cap, the hands folded on the shrunken breast. Grey from slimy horror, Gustave raised himself up, and went over to look for the eyes. When he saw them pressed down with pennies, he reeled back and vomited into the grate. And blind, and sick, and loathing, he stumbled up-stairs.

But as he passed by Madame Jahn's bedroom the corpse came out to meet him, with the eyes closed and the pennies pressing them down. Then, at last, reeking and dabbled with sweat, with his tongue lolling out, and the spittle running down his beard, Gustave breathed:

"Are you alive?"

"No, no!" wailed the thing, with a burst of awful weeping; "I have been dead many days."

The Interval

MRS. WILTON passed through a little alley leading from one of the gates which are around Regent's Park, and came out on the wide and quiet street. She walked along slowly, peering anxiously from side to side so as not to overlook the number. She pulled her furs closer round her; after her years in India this London damp seemed very harsh. Still, it was not a fog to-day. A dense haze, gray and tinged ruddy, lay between the houses, sometimes blowing with a little wet kiss against the face. Mrs. Wilton's hair and eyelashes and her furs were powdered with tiny drops. But there was nothing in the weather to blur the sight; she could see the faces of people some distance off and read the signs on the shops.

Before the door of a dealer in antiques and second-hand furniture she paused and looked through the shabby uncleaned window at an unassorted heap of things, many of them of great value. She read the Polish name fastened on the pane in white letters.

"Yes; this is the place."

She opened the door, which met her entrance with an ill-tempered jangle. From somewhere in the black depths of the shop the dealer came forward. He had a clammy white face, with a sparse black beard, and wore a skull cap and spectacles. Mrs. Wilton spoke to him in a low voice.

A look of complicity, of cunning, perhaps of irony, passed through the dealer's cynical and sad eyes. But he bowed gravely and respectfully.

"Yes, she is here, madam. Whether she will see you or not I do not know. She is not always well; she has her moods. And then, we have to be so careful. The police——Not that they would touch a lady like you. But the poor alien has not much chance these days."

Mrs. Wilton followed him to the back of the shop, where there was a winding staircase. She knocked over a few things in her passage and stooped to pick them up, but the dealer kept muttering, "It does not matter—surely it does not matter." He lit a candle.

"You must go up these stairs. They are very dark; be careful. When you come to a door, open it and go straight in."

He stood at the foot of the stairs holding the light high above his head and she ascended.

The room was not very large, and it seemed very ordinary.

There were some flimsy, uncomfortable chairs in gilt and red. Two large palms were in corners. Under a glass cover on the table was a view of Rome. The room had not a business-like look, thought Mrs. Wilton; there was no suggestion of the office or waiting-room where people came and went all day; yet you would not say that it was a private room which was lived in. There were no books or papers about; every chair was in the place it had been placed when the room was last swept; there was no fire and it was very cold.

To the right of the window was a door covered with a plush curtain. Mrs. Wilton sat down near the table and watched this door. She thought it must be through it that the soothsayer would come forth. She laid her hands listlessly one on top of the other on the table. This must be the tenth seer she had consulted since Hugh had been killed. She thought them over. No, this must be the eleventh. She had forgotten that frightening man in Paris who said he had been a priest. Yet of them all it was only he who had told her anything definite. But even he could do no more than tell the past. He told of her marriage; he even had the duration of it right—twenty-one months. He told too of their time in India—at least, knew that her husband had been a soldier, and said he had been on service in the "colonies." On the whole, though, he had been as unsatisfactory as the others. None of them had given her the consolation she sought. She did not want to be told of the past. If Hugh was gone forever, then with him had gone all her love of living, her courage, all her better self. She wanted to be lifted out of the despair, the dazed aimless drifting from day to day, longing at night for the morning, and in the morning for the fall of night, which had been her life since his death. If somebody could assure her that it was not all over, that he was somewhere, not too far away, unchanged from what he had been here, with his crisp hair and rather slow smile and lean brown face, that he saw her sometimes, that he had not forgotten her...

"Oh, Hugh, darling!"

When she looked up again the woman was sitting there before her. Mrs. Wilton had not heard her come in. With her experience, wide enough now, of seers and fortunetellers of all kinds, she saw at once that this woman was different from the others. She was used to the quick appraising look, the attempts, sometimes clumsy, but often cleverly disguised, to collect some fragments of information whereupon to erect a plausible vision. But this woman looked as if she took it out of herself.

Not that her appearance suggested intercourse with the spiritual world more than the others had done; it suggested that, in fact, considerably less. Some of the others were frail, yearning, evaporated creatures, and the ex-priest in Paris had something terrible and condemned in his look. He might well sup with the devil, that man, and probably did in some way or other.

But this was a little fat, weary-faced woman about fifty, who only did not look like a cook because she looked more like a sempstress. Her black dress was all covered with white threads. Mrs. Wilton looked at her with some embarrassment. It seemed more reasonable to be asking a woman like this about altering a gown than about intercourse with the dead. That seemed even absurd in such a very commonplace presence. The woman seemed timid, and oppressed: she breathed heavily and kept rubbing her dingy hands, which looked moist, one over the other; she was always wetting her lips, and coughed with a little dry cough. But in her these signs of nervous exhaustion suggested overwork in a close atmosphere, bending too close over the sewing-machine. Her uninteresting hair, like a rat's pelt, was eked out with a false addition of another color. Some threads had got into her hair too.

Her harried, uneasy look caused Mrs. Wilton to ask compassionately: "Are you much worried by the police?"

"Oh, the police! Why don't they leave us alone? You never know who comes to see you. Why don't they leave me alone? I'm a good woman. I only think. What I do is no harm to any one."...

She continued in an uneven querulous voice, always rubbing her hands together nervously. She seemed to the visitor to be talking at random, just gabbling, like children do sometimes before they fall asleep.

"I wanted to explain—-" hesitated Mrs. Wilton.

But the woman, with her head pressed close against the back of the chair, was staring beyond her at the wall. Her face had lost whatever little expression it had; it was blank and stupid. When she spoke it was very slowly and her voice was guttural.

"Can't you see him? It seems strange to me that you can't see him. He is so near you. He is passing his arm round your shoulders."

This was a frequent gesture of Hugh's. And indeed at that moment she felt that somebody was very near her, bending over her. She was enveloped in tenderness. Only a very thin veil, she felt, prevented her from seeing. But the woman saw. She was describing Hugh minutely, even the little things like the burn on his right hand.

"Is he happy? Oh, ask him does he love me?"

The result was so far beyond anything she had hoped for that she was stunned. She could only stammer the first thing that came into her head. "Does he love me?"

"He loves you. He won't answer, but he loves you. He wants me to make you see him; he is disappointed, I think, because I can't. But I can't unless you do it yourself."

After a while she said:

"I think you will see him again. You think of nothing else. He is very close to us now."

Then she collapsed, and fell into a heavy sleep and lay there motionless, hardly breathing. Mrs. Wilton put some notes on the table and stole out on tip-toe.

She seemed to remember that downstairs in the dark shop the dealer with the waxen face detained her to show some old silver and jewelry and such like. But she did not come to herself, she had no precise recollection of anything, till she found herself entering a church near Portland Place. It was an unlikely act in her normal moments. Why did she go in there? She acted like one walking in her sleep.

The church was old and dim, with high black pews. There was nobody there. Mrs. Wilton sat down in one of the pews and bent forward with her face in her hands.

After a few minutes she saw that a soldier had come in noiselessly and placed himself about half-a-dozen rows ahead of her. He never turned round; but presently she was struck by something familiar in the figure. First she thought vaguely that the soldier looked like her Hugh. Then, when he put up his hand, she saw who it was.

She hurried out of the pew and ran towards him. "Oh, Hugh, Hugh, have you come back?"

He looked round with a smile. He had not been killed. It was all a mistake. He was going to speak...

Footsteps sounded hollow in the empty church. She turned and glanced down the dim aisle.

It was an old sexton or verger who approached. "I thought I heard you call," he said.

"I was speaking to my husband." But Hugh was nowhere to be seen.

"He was here a moment ago." She looked about in anguish. "He must have gone to the door."

"There's nobody here," said the old man gently. "Only you and me. Ladies are often taken funny since the war. There was one in here yesterday afternoon said she was married in this church and her husband had promised to meet her here. Perhaps you were married here?"

"No," said Mrs. Wilton, desolately. "I was married in India."

It might have been two or three days after that, when she went into a small Italian restaurant in the Bayswater district. She often went out for her meals now: she had developed an exhausting cough, and she found that it somehow became less troublesome when she was in a public place looking at strange faces. In her flat there were all the things that Hugh had used; the trunks and bags still had his name on them with the labels of places where they had been together. They were like stabs. In the restaurant, people came and went, many soldiers too among them, just glancing at her in her comer.

This day, as it chanced, she was rather late and there was nobody there. She was very tired. She nibbled at the food they brought her. She could almost have cried from tiredness and loneliness and the ache in her heart.

Then suddenly he was before her, sitting there opposite at the table. It was as it was in the days of their engagement, when they used sometimes to lunch at restaurants. He was not in uniform. He smiled at her and urged her to eat, just as he used in those days...

I met her that afternoon as she was crossing Kensington Gardens, and she told me about it.

"I have been with Hugh." She seemed most happy.

"Did he say anything?"

"N-no. Yes. I think he did, but I could not quite hear. My head was so very tired. The next time —-"

I did not see her for some time after that. She found, I think, that by going to places where she had once seen him—the old church, the little restaurant—she was more certain to see him again. She never saw him at home. But in the street or the park he would often walk along beside her. Once he saved her from being run over. She said she actually felt his hand grabbing her arm, suddenly, when the car was nearly upon her.

She had given me the address of the clairvoyant: and it is through that strange woman that I know—or seem to know—what followed.

Mrs. Wilton was not exactly ill last winter, not so ill, at least, as to keep to her bedroom. But she was very thin, and her great handsome eyes always seemed to be staring at some point beyond, searching. There was a look in them that seamen's eyes sometimes have when they are drawing on a coast of which they are not very certain. She lived almost in solitude: she hardly ever saw anybody except when they sought her out. To those who were anxious about her she laughed and said she was very well.

One sunny morning she was lying awake, waiting for the maid to bring her tea. The shy London sunlight peeped through the blinds. The room had a fresh and happy look.

When she heard the door open she thought that the maid had come in. Then she saw that Hugh was standing at the foot of the bed. He was in uniform this time, and looked as he had looked the day he went away.

"Oh, Hugh, speak to me! Will you not say just one word?"

He smiled and threw back his head, just as he used to in the old days at her mother's house when he wanted to call her out of the room without attracting the attention of the others. He moved towards the door, still signing to her to follow him. He picked up her slippers on his way and held them out to her as if he wanted her to put them on. She slipped out of bed hastily...

It is strange that when they came to look through her things after her death the slippers could never be found.

THE END

CPSIA information can be obtained at www.ICGtesting.com
Printed in the USA
LVOW101911030812

292856LV00001B/345/P